WILD ABOUT ANIMALS

TIGERS

By Emma Huddleston

Kaleidoscope
Minneapolis, MN

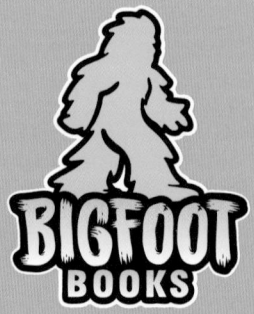

The Quest for Discovery Never Ends

This edition first published in 2020 by Kaleidoscope Publishing, Inc.

No part of this publication may be reproduced in whole or in part without written permission of the publisher.

For information regarding permission, write to
Kaleidoscope Publishing, Inc.
6012 Blue Circle Drive
Minnetonka, MN 55343

Library of Congress Control Number
2019938856

ISBN
978-1-64519-010-3 (library bound)
978-1-64494-252-9 (paperback)
978-1-64519-110-0 (ebook)

Text copyright © 2020 by Kaleidoscope Publishing, Inc. All-Star Sports, Bigfoot Books, and associated logos are trademarks and/or registered trademarks of Kaleidoscope Publishing, Inc.

Printed in the United States of America.

Bigfoot lurks within one of the images in this book. It's up to you to find him!

TABLE OF CONTENTS

Chapter 1: The Largest Cat **4**

Chapter 2: Strong Hunter **10**

Chapter 3: Solitary Life **16**

Chapter 4: Protecting Tigers **20**

Beyond the Book 28
Research Ninja 29
Further Resources 30
Glossary 31
Index 32
Photo Credits 32
About the Author 32

CHAPTER 1

The Largest Cat

Muddy water flows down the river. Tall green grass fills the bank. It is the Ganges River in India. A male Bengal tiger walks in the forest near the river. He has a bright orange coat. White and black stripes cover it. Every tiger has a unique stripe pattern. No two tigers look the same.

FUN FACT
Tigers can live ten years in the wild and eighteen in zoos.

He comes to the edge of the river. Some big cats are afraid of water. Tigers are not. Sometimes he hunts crocodiles. Other times he relaxes in the water. Now, he swims across. He is **stalking** deer. They are on the other side.

There are more Bengal tigers in the wild than any other kind of tiger.

A tiger's coat helps camouflage it in the grass.

The pattern of his coat acts as **camouflage**. He hides in the grass. The stripes make his body difficult to see. They look like shadows.

Tigers are the largest cats in the world. This tiger weighs 480 pounds (220 kg). His head and body are 6 feet (1.8 m) long. His tail is 3 feet (0.9 m) long. The grass is barely taller than his head. He moves slowly. His body brushes the plants.

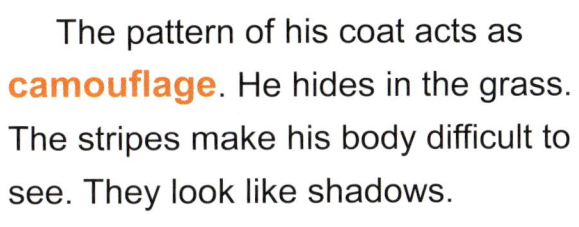

PARTS OF A
TIGER

camouflaging coat

long teeth

scratchy tongue

retractable claws

webbed toes for swimming

8

He follows the deer to an open area. A few trees sway in the wind. He tries to get close. One of the deer hears him. She makes a chirping sound. All the deer run away. The tiger is not close enough to catch them. Only 10 percent of hunts end in success. He will hunt again later.

The Bengal tiger is India's national animal.

CHAPTER 2

Siberian tigers have thick coats to protect them from the cold and snow.

Strong Hunter

Snow covers the ground in Russia. A Siberian tigress climbs a small hill. Her pale coat has fewer stripes than other tigers. This helps her blend into the snow. The tigress has a layer of fat under her thick coat. This helps her stay warm. Siberian tigers are the largest tiger species. Males weigh up to 660 pounds (300 kg). This tigress weighs 370 pounds (167 kg). With her tail, she is 8.5 feet (2.6 m) long.

FUN FACT
Tigers can leap up to 32 feet (9.8 m).

    She hunts once or twice a week. The sun goes down. It is time. Her eyes are made for night vision. She spots an antelope in the trees. She stalks it patiently. She follows it for a long time. Her curved claws scratch a rock. She **retracts** them. This keeps them sharp for hunting. Her large padded paws make prints in the ground. White snow mixes with the brown dirt.

She sneaks close to her **prey**. Her tail is not hanging loose and relaxed. It twitches side to side. She is ready to fight. Suddenly, she pounces. Her long back legs push her into the air. Her paws land on the antelope's back. She knocks it to the ground. She uses her teeth. She is a strong hunter.

13 feet (4 m)

HOW BIG ARE SIBERIAN TIGERS?

Siberian tigers can grow up to 13 FEET (4 M) long!

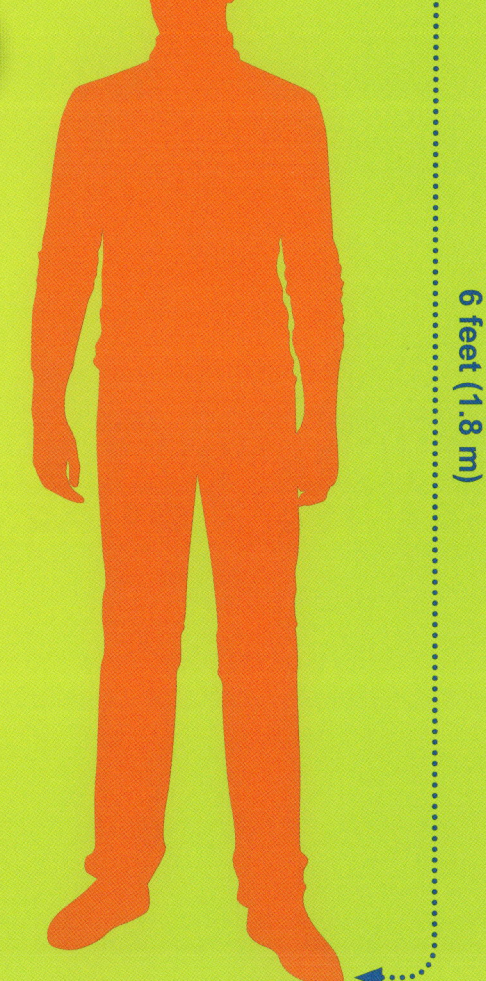

6 feet (1.8 m)

The tigress eats her food. She can eat up to 60 pounds (27 kg) in one meal. But normally she eats 12 pounds (5 kg) at a time. Her rough tongue is like sandpaper. It scrapes meat off bones. When she is full, she stands up. She covers the food with dirt and leaves. This hides it from other animals. She comes back when she is hungry. She does this until all the meat is gone. It takes days for her to finish this food.

WHO WOULD WIN A FIGHT BETWEEN A TIGER AND A LION?

In the wild, a tiger could lose a fight with a lion. Tigers live alone. Lions live in groups. They could work together to beat one tiger. However, a tiger would win against a lion one-on-one. Tigers are larger. They are used to fighting alone. They fight to kill.

Siberian tigers are also called Amur tigers.

CHAPTER 3

Solitary Life

A Sumatran tiger walks through the jungle. He weighs 265 pounds (120 kg). He is the smallest kind of tiger. His dark orange coat helps him blend in with his surroundings. Sumatran tigers are only found on Sumatra, an island in Indonesia. The jungle is full of tall plants. Big leaves move in the breeze. He has long fur on the sides of his face. This protects him from jungle plants.

The **solitary** tiger marks his territory. He pees and scratches the ground. The strong smell can last forty days. He wants other animals to know this is his area. Sometimes he roars. This challenges other tigers from a distance. He also uses his roar to attract a mate. Mating is usually the only time he is not alone.

FUN FACT
A tiger's roar can be heard from 2 miles (3 km) away!

There are fewer than 400 Sumatran tigers left in the wild.

A tigress gives birth to a litter. Two cubs are born. They weigh 2 pounds (1 kg) at birth. She has to protect them. Half of tiger cubs die in the first few months. Some are attacked by larger animals. Others get sick. The tigress and her cubs live in a **den**. She gives them all her attention for two years. She raises them alone.

Each tiger has a unique smell. Cubs can track their mother's scent.

Tigers have scent glands between their toes, under their tail, and on their face.

The cubs stay in the den for two months. Their mother eats extra food. They drink her milk. One grows stronger than the other. He wrestles his sister. After two months, the cubs join their mother on hunting trips. She teaches them to kill pigs. The cubs growl. They chase each other. They practice hunting. The tigress sleeps. They try to sneak up on her. They jump on her. She **chuffles** at the cubs.

CHAPTER 4

Protecting Tigers

Claudio is an environmental activist. Activists stand up for what they believe. They spread news. Claudio cares about helping animals and the environment.

Claudio is worried about tigers. They are **endangered**. People watch tigers perform in shows. Sometimes the tigers are treated badly. Breeders make money off tigers. They might hurt the ones that don't look as nice. In many states, it's legal to own tigers as pets. But tigers can be uncomfortable or stressed in **captivity**. They can be dangerous. Claudio tells people to think about the tigers first. If they want to see a tiger, the best place to go is India. Tigers live in the wild there. They have plenty of space. The Indian government protects them.

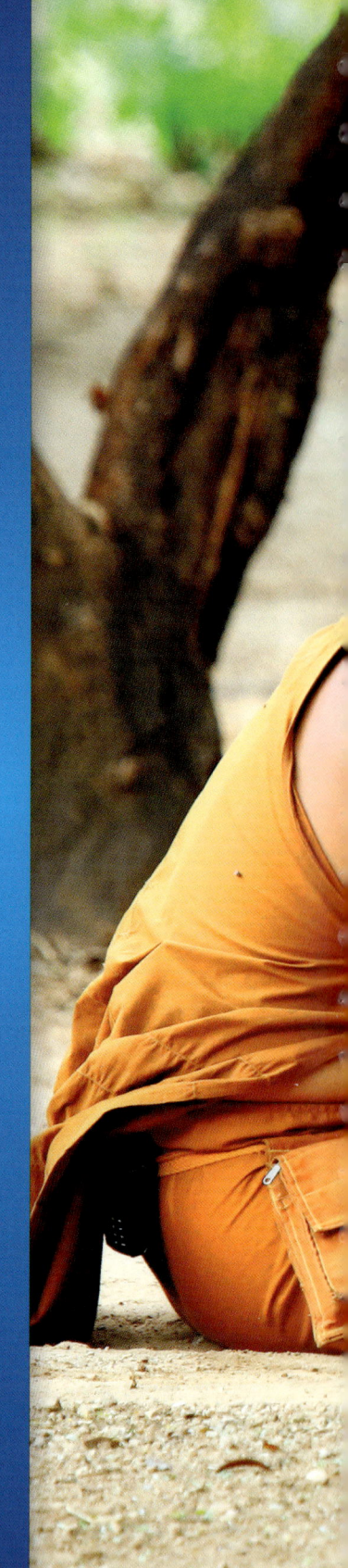

In 2016, the famous Tiger Temple in Thailand had 137 tigers taken by the government. The temple was accused of hurting and illegally breeding tigers for the black market.

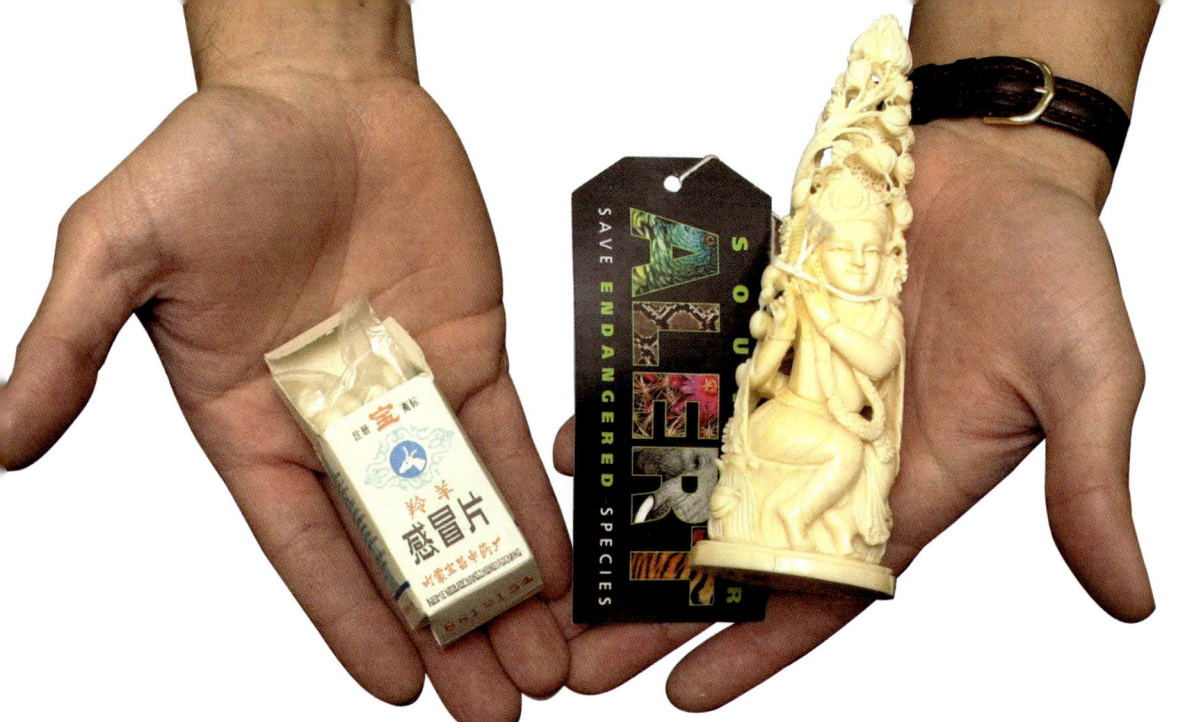

Many traditional Chinese medicines use tiger parts. This leaves tigers in danger of being poached.

TIGER RESERVES

The Indian government is trying to protect tigers. There are fifty tiger reserves in India. There are also national parks and wildlife sanctuaries. These places help protect tigers. People can visit and see tigers on tours. But they should make sure the tours are respectful of tigers.

Poaching is another threat to tigers. It makes Claudio sad. Tigers have beautiful coats. People poach them to make products like rugs. In the 1970s, India created laws against shooting tigers. Other countries made laws, too. They were against selling tiger products. Unfortunately, tigers are still poached today. More than 100 are killed every year. A dead adult male tiger can be illegally sold for $10,000.

Tiger reserves like Ranthambore National Park in India allow tourists to view tigers in their natural habitat.

Where Do Tigers Live?

Penny is a zookeeper at the San Diego Zoo in California. She and the zoo want to help tigers. Tigers live in different forest **habitats** in Asia. They live in small, scattered areas. But people move into places where tigers used to live. This habitat loss threatens tigers. It's also dangerous for people.

FUN FACT
White tigers are not a species. They are Bengal tigers bred to be white.

Tigers suffer from habitat loss.

Penny watches tigers play in the water. They splash each other. Penny smiles. Zoos help tigers. They protect them. Breeding programs help the population grow. Penny teaches people about tigers. She cares for them. Sometimes she puts different scents on rocks in their habitats. They are curious. New smells are interesting to tigers.

The sun is bright. Penny brings the tigers food. The tigers play. She hopes people will protect them. She wants them to survive for years to come.

There are fewer than 4,000 tigers left in the wild. Humans can help change that.

BEYOND
THE BOOK

After reading the book, it's time to think about what you learned. Try the following exercises to jumpstart your ideas.

THINK

DIFFERENT SOURCES. Think about what types of sources you could find on tigers. What could you find in an encyclopedia? What could you learn at a zoo? How could each of the sources be useful in its own way?

CREATE

SHARPEN YOUR RESEARCH SKILLS. Tigers are endangered animals. Where could you go in the library to find more information about endangered species? Who could you talk to who might know more? Create a research plan. Write a paragraph about your next steps.

SHARE

WHAT'S YOUR OPINION? In many states, it's legal to own a tiger as a pet. Some people think tigers should only live in the wild. Do you agree or disagree with this position? Use evidence from the text to support your answer. Share your position and evidence with a friend. Does your friend agree with you?

GROW

DRAWING CONNECTIONS. Create a drawing that shows the connections between tigers and their habitats. What makes a tiger well-suited to its habitat? How can changing habitats harm tigers? How does learning about these connections help you better understand tigers?

RESEARCH NINJA

Visit www.ninjaresearcher.com/0103 to learn how to take your research skills and book report writing to the next level!

RESEARCH

DIGITAL LITERACY TOOLS

SEARCH LIKE A PRO
Learn about how to use search engines to find useful websites.

FACT OR FAKE?
Discover how you can tell a trusted website from an untrustworthy resource.

TEXT DETECTIVE
Explore how to zero in on the information you need most.

SHOW YOUR WORK
Research responsibly—learn how to cite sources.

WRITE

GET TO THE POINT
Learn how to express your main ideas.

PLAN OF ATTACK
Learn prewriting exercises and create an outline.

DOWNLOADABLE REPORT FORMS

Further Resources

BOOKS

Hansen, Grace. *Siberian Tigers*. Abdo Publishing, 2019.

Markert, Jenny. *Tigers*. The Child's World, 2015.

Murray, Julie. *Tigers*. Abdo Publishing, 2013.

WEBSITES

Factsurfer.com gives you a safe, fun way to find more information.

1. Go to www.factsurfer.com.
2. Enter "Tigers" into the search box and click.
3. Select your book cover to see a list of related websites.

Glossary

camouflage: Camouflage is a covering that blends in with the environment. Tigers' coats act as camouflage to hide them while they hunt.

captivity: Living in a limited space is living in captivity. Animals in captivity often live in zoos or as people's pets.

chuffles: When a tiger chuffles, it makes a noise that mixes growling and sniffing. A tigress chuffles at her cubs.

den: A den is a hollow or cave used by wild animals. The tigress lived in a den with her cubs to protect them.

endangered: A species is endangered when its population in the wild is very low. Tigers are endangered because of poaching and habitat loss.

habitats: Habitats are places where animals live. Tigers live in different forest habitats in Asia.

poaching: Poaching is illegal hunting. India has made laws to protect tigers, but some people are still poaching them.

prey: Prey is an animal that another animal eats. Antelope and deer are prey for tigers.

retracts: An item that retracts is pulled back or pulled into something. The tigress retracts her claws into her paw, like a house cat.

solitary: A solitary being lives on its own or away from others. Tigers are solitary animals.

stalking: Stalking is following prey during the hunt. Tigers hunt by stalking their prey.

Index

Bengal tigers, 4–9, 25

camouflage, 7, 8, 10, 16
captivity, 20
claws, 8, 11
coats, 4, 7, 8, 10, 16, 23
cubs, 18–19

eating, 14, 19
endangered tigers, 20–24

habitat loss, 24
hunting, 5–9, 11–12, 19

India, 4, 20–23, 24
Indonesia, 16, 24

poaching, 23

reserves, 22
rivers, 4–5
Russia, 10, 24

Siberian tigers, 10–14
size, 7, 10, 12–13, 16, 18
Sumatran tigers, 16

tongues, 8, 14

where tigers live, 4, 10, 16, 18–19, 22, 24
white tigers, 25

zoos, 4, 24–27

PHOTO CREDITS

The images in this book are reproduced through the courtesy of: ehtesham/Shutterstock Images, front cover; Sarawut Aiemsinsuk/Shutterstock Images, p. 3; Anuradha Marwah/Shutterstock Images, pp. 4–5, 23; Joe McDonald/Shutterstock Images, pp. 6–7; neelsky/Shutterstock Images, p. 7; Martin Mecnarowski/Shutterstock Images, p. 8; Michal Ninger/Shutterstock Images, p. 9; Vaclav Sebek/Shutterstock Images, pp. 10–11; Popova Valeriya/Shutterstock Images, pp. 12–13 (tiger); Chipmunk131/Shutterstock Images, p. 13 (person); Alexei Merinov Krr/Shutterstock Images, p. 14; belizar/Shutterstock Images, p. 15; Stepan Kapl/Shutterstock Images, p. 16; neelsky/Shutterstock Images, p. 17; Bildagentur Zoonar GmbH/Shutterstock Images, pp. 18, 19; Kamonrat/Shutterstock Images, pp. 20–21; Rui Vieira/PA Images/Getty Images, p. 22; Red Line Editorial, p. 24; Ondrej Prosicky/Shutterstock Images, p. 25; hxdbzxy/Shutterstock Images, pp. 26–27; Anan Kaewkhammul/Shutterstock Images, p. 30.

ABOUT THE AUTHOR

Emma Huddleston has written books about science, sports, animals, and more. She thinks animals are fascinating. When she isn't writing, she enjoys reading and swing dancing. She lives in the Twin Cities with her husband.